NASCAR Safety on the Track

By Mark Stewart & Mike Kennedy

Lerner Publications Company/Minneapolis

The publisher wishes to thank science teachers Amy K. Tilmont and Jeffrey R. Garside of the Rumson Country Day School in Rumson, New Jersey, for their help in preparing this book.

Lerner Publications Company
A division of Lerner Publishing Group, Inc.
241 First Avenue North
Minneapolis, MN 55401 U.S.A.

Website address: www.lernerbooks.com

All photos provided by Getty Images.

Library of Congress Cataloging-in-Publication Data

Stewart, Mark, 1960-
NASCAR safety on the track / By Mark Stewart & Mike Kennedy.
p. cm. — (The science of NASCAR)
Includes index.
ISBN 978-0-8225-8742-2 (lib. bdg. : alk. paper)
1. Automobile racing—Accidents. 2. Automobiles, Racing—Safety appliances.
3. Automobile racing—Safety measures. 4. NASCAR (Association)
I. Kennedy, Mike (Mike William), 1965- II. Title.
GV1029.13.S743 2008
796.72—dc22   2007024888

Manufactured in the United States of America
1 2 3 4 5 6 – DP – 13 12 11 10 09 08

Contents

Introduction

Auto racing can be a challenging sport. No matter how careful drivers and mechanics are, something can always go wrong. Accidents happen. Even though most drivers are unhurt, no one wants to be in a wreck.

NASCAR puts a lot of thought into safety. Every day, medical experts, scientists, and engineers explore new ways to keep drivers, pit crews, and fans out of harm's way. This book looks at their greatest challenges and their best solutions.

ACCIDENTS CAN HAPPEN IN NASCAR RACES. THAT IS WHY THE SCIENCE OF SAFETY IS SO IMPORTANT. DRIVERS ARE ABLE TO WALK AWAY FROM EVEN THE WORST CRASHES.

4

TOP: DRIVER KEVIN HARVICK *(LEFT)* AND A CREW MEMBER WATCH HIS CAR BEING FIXED. *ABOVE:* A TEAM OF ENGINEERS WORKS TO SOLVE PROBLEMS DURING PRACTICE.

Chapter One: Crunch Time

Most wrecks begin in one of two ways. A driver may do something unexpected. Or something may go wrong with a car. In each case, the other drivers have only an instant to make a decision and act. Drivers must have great skill to avoid a problem at 180 miles per hour. They also need luck from time to time. Unfortunately, sometimes there is nothing a driver can do. That's when a car's safety systems take over.

DAVE BLANEY'S CAR SLIDES TOWARD THE WALL DURING A 2007 RACE IN NEW HAMPSHIRE. AT TIMES LIKE THESE, DRIVERS DEPEND ON THEIR SAFETY SYSTEMS

TOP: WHEN ONE CAR LOSES
CONTROL, IT CAN CAUSE OTHERS
TO SWERVE AND SKID. *LEFT:* DRIVER
MIKE SKINNER PUTS ON HIS SAFETY
HARNESS. THIS IS AN IMPORTANT
PART OF A CAR'S SAFETY SYSTEM.

Mission Control

Race cars are built to travel at high speeds. Their bodies are designed so that air passes over them smoothly. The air also pushes down on the car. This helps keep the wheels on the track. The cars' tires are made to stay on the track through long turns. At all times, a driver must be in control.

Do the Math

A race car weighs more than 3,400 pounds without the driver. The driver tips the scales at 180 pounds. A full tank of gas weighs 110 pounds. What is the total weight of the car with a driver behind the wheel ready to race?

(answer on page 48)

DAVID STREMME LOOKS CLOSELY AT ONE OF THE TIRES THAT HE WILL USE.

The faster a race car travels, the more it wants to keep going straight. When drivers turn the steering wheel, they are fighting against this force. They need the grip—the friction—between the tires and the track to be strong. Strong friction will keep them from sliding as they go through sharp turns. Friction helps them as they swerve to avoid other drivers.

Why does a car want to continue in a straight line when it takes a curve? The car is experiencing momentum. This is a combination of the car's speed and its weight. Momentum is one of the laws of physics. Physics is the science that explains how objects in motion behave.

ABOVE: AS CARS DRIVE THROUGH A TURN, THEY DEPEND ON THE FRICTION THEIR TIRES CREATE. TOP: FRICTION CREATES HEAT. THIS TIRE BECAME SO HOT THAT IT MELTED THE PAINT ON THE TRACK!

9

Slick Stuff

Race cars lose friction when the track surface becomes slick. This happens when it rains. Drivers know to slow down in bad weather. But slickness also can come from oil on the track. Drivers may not have time to slow down if oil begins leaking from another car's engine. If oil spills on the track, the cars that drive through it start sliding. For an instant, they lose control. The moment oil hits the track, a race official waves a yellow flag. The yellow flag stands for caution. The cars must slow down. A safety crew cleans up the mess.

WHEN OIL CAUSES CARS TO LOSE CONTROL, NASCAR OFFICIALS WAVE THE YELLOW CAUTION FLAG.

Cars can also slip on air. When they are racing close together single file, the air pressure above the cars is high. It pushes down the cars on the track. Below the cars, less air flows, and air pressure is lower. If a car is bumped, air may rush underneath it. The air pressure may change suddenly. The tires may lose their grip for just a second. But in that time, a car can spin out of control or even rise into the air.

In the Mix

Why is motor oil so dangerous on a race track? The oil is made to reduce the friction between a car engine's metal parts. An oil spill lowers the friction between the tires and the track surface. This can cause the tires to slip.

LEFT: A MEMBER OF ELLIOTT SADLER'S CREW SWEEPS WATER FROM THE PIT AREA AFTER A RAINSTORM. *ABOVE:* A CAR LOSES CONTACT WITH THE ROAD WHEN TOO MUCH AIR GETS UNDERNEATH IT.

See for Yourself

To avoid a wreck, NASCAR drivers must see a problem the second it starts. To get an idea how quickly drivers think, try this experiment.

- Take three old tennis balls. Using three different colored markers, make a large dot on each tennis ball.
- Have a friend stand five big steps away from you. Have the friend hold the balls where you can't see them.
- Ask your friend to quickly and gently toss one of the balls to you underhand.
- Try to call out the color of the dot on the ball before you catch it.
- Repeat this action several times. Switch roles with your friend. You will get better the more you play.

It takes about a second to recognize which ball is being thrown to you. NASCAR drivers often have even less time to avoid trouble.

Airborne

In 1993, Rusty Wallace crashed during the Daytona 500 in Florida. He crashed again that year at Talladega in Alabama. In the first crash, two other cars ran into each other and then smashed into Wallace. The second crash was partly his fault. Dale Earnhardt Sr. tried to pass Wallace at the end of the race. But Wallace moved to block him, and the two cars hit. Both times, Wallace's car lost contact with the road and tumbled across the track. Fans nicknamed Wallace Old Rubberhead. But nothing was funny about his crashes. After Wallace's crashes, NASCAR ordered that every car had to have special safety flaps on its roof. They open automatically during an accident to keep cars on the track and out of the air.

RUSTY WALLACE SMILES BEFORE A RACE. NASCAR MADE IMPORTANT SAFETY CHANGES AFTER HIS CRASHES.

Shoptalk

"I'M VERY CONCERNED ABOUT SAFETY."

—DRIVER RUSTY WALLACE

NASCAR drivers are very good at what they do. After losing control, they can use their braking and steering skills to stay on the track. Unfortunately, sometimes they fail. They may be traveling too fast. Or another car might hit them from behind. Sometimes all a driver can do is hold on to the steering wheel and hope for the best. At these times, the drivers benefit from the knowledge of people who have studied the forces at work in a wreck.

WHEN CARS SPIN OUT, DRIVERS NEED TO KNOW THEY CAN DEPEND ON THEIR SAFETY SYSTEMS.

DRIVERS AND NASCAR OFFICIALS USE
COMPUTERS TO IMPROVE SAFETY WHEN
THERE IS AN ACCIDENT ON THE TRACK.
RYAN NEWMAN (TOP) WORKS ON A LAPTOP
BETWEEN PRACTICE RUNS. A NASCAR
OFFICIAL (LEFT) CHECKS HIS FACTS AND
FIGURES ON A COMPUTER.

Bodywork

NASCAR is very interested in keeping drivers safe. NASCAR designers study the many forces involved in racing. These include the forces on the human body. Bones and muscles are very strong. Body organs, such as the brain and the heart, are not. NASCAR designs its cars, tracks, and equipment to protect all parts of the human body.

How safe is it to be a NASCAR driver? Fans are amazed when they see a driver walk away from an accident. The truth is that very few drivers suffer injuries. They are back behind the wheel in time for the next race.

DRIVER STEVE PARK WAS NOT HURT WHEN HIS CAR (CENTER) WAS HIT FROM BOTH SIDES DURING THIS RACE.

ABOVE: TONY STEWART'S CAR WAS UNABLE TO FINISH THE 2007 LIFELOCK 400 IN KANSAS, BUT HE WAS READY TO GO FOR THE NEXT RACE. *RIGHT:* DRIVERS JUAN PABLO MONTOYA *(LEFT)* AND KEVIN HARVICK FEEL GOOD ENOUGH AFTER THIS ACCIDENT TO ARGUE ABOUT WHOSE FAULT IT WAS. *BELOW:* THE HUMAN BODY DOES A GOOD JOB OF PROTECTING ORGANS SUCH AS THE HEART *(SHOWN IN RED).* NASCAR DESIGNERS LOOK FOR WAYS TO KEEP THE BODY EVEN SAFER.

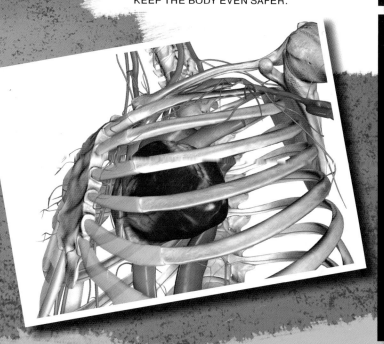

Do the Math

Drivers work out between races to strengthen their bodies. Let's say a driver does arm lifts with 150-pound weights and leg lifts with 250 pounds. What is the total amount of weight lifted?

(answer on page 48)

Mind Readers

The brain is in charge of the human body. The skull gives protection to the brain. As further protection, fluid surrounds the brain inside the skull.

The helmet is a driver's most important piece of safety equipment. NASCAR helmets are molded to fit each driver's head. Soft inner padding slows the speed of the head during a sudden blow. A hard outer shell spreads out the force. This helps the driver's skull protect the brain. The shell and padding work together to prevent serious head injuries.

LEFT: JUAN PABLO MONTOYA CHECKS THE FIT OF HIS HELMET BEFORE A RACE. *ABOVE:* NASCAR HELMET DESIGN HAS COME A LONG WAY SINCE RICHARD PETTY *(RIGHT)* HELPED TO TEST HELMETS IN THE 1970s.

A driver's skull and its fluid, as well as the padding of a helmet, shield the brain. These protections cushion any blow a driver receives. Head injuries are unusual in NASCAR racing.

ABOVE LEFT: DRIVER DENNY HAMLIN EXPLAINS TO A YOUNG FAN HOW HIS HELMET WORKS. *BELOW LEFT:* HELMETS MUST BE ADJUSTED TO FIT EACH DRIVER PERFECTLY.

Body Language

When the brain moves suddenly inside the skull, the injury is called a concussion. A concussion can take place when a driver's head receives a blow. It can also occur when a car stops moving suddenly.

See for Yourself

How fragile is the human brain? To understand better, try this experiment.

- Place an egg inside an empty plastic mayonnaise jar. (Be sure the jar is made of plastic, not glass.) Fill the jar with enough vinegar to cover the egg. Screw the lid back on, and wait two days.
- Empty out the vinegar, but keep in the egg. Replace the old vinegar with fresh vinegar. Wait two more days. The eggshell should dissolve, but the egg should keep its oval shape. This is your "brain."
- Empty out the vinegar again, keeping the egg inside the jar. Fill the jar with water but not all the way to the top. Screw the lid on tight. This is your "skull."
- Tell anyone around you to stand back. Throw the jar in front of you, high in the air, so that the jar hits the ground with a thud.

Did the egg survive? If so, your "brain" was lucky. You only suffered a concussion. If your egg broke, your brain will need emergency surgery.

Super Doors

"We believe that drivers are safer than ever."
—MIKE HELTON, PRESIDENT OF NASCAR

NASCAR is always looking for new ways to protect its drivers when accidents happen. To take in energy from a sideways crash, all cars have special doors made with steel plates. They keep the driver's left side from being injured. The car's frame has double rails on this side to add even more strength and protection.

TOP: NASCAR'S NEW DOORS PROTECT DRIVERS LIKE DAVID GILLILAND (NO. 38). LEFT: SAFETY IS VERY IMPORTANT TO NASCAR PRESIDENT MIKE HELTON (LEFT) AND ALL-TIME GREAT DRIVER BOBBY ALLISON.

21

Chapter Three: Inside Safety

Have you ever seen an old racing photo from the 1950s? If so, look carefully at the safety equipment the drivers wore. Besides a helmet, there isn't much to see. Back then, the drivers wore blue jeans, a T-shirt, sneakers, and sunglasses. NASCAR has come a long way since then. Modern drivers have the best science and technology on their side. Behind the wheel, safety comes first.

ABOVE: DRIVER JUNIOR JOHNSON DID NOT WEAR MUCH SAFETY GEAR WHEN HE WON THE 1960 DAYTONA 500. *RIGHT:* MODERN DRIVERS LIKE CARL EDWARDS ARE PROTECTED FROM HEAD TO TOE.

TOP: NASCAR DRIVERS COUNT ON HELMETS, GLOVES, AND SAFETY HARNESSES TO KEEP THEM SAFE. *ABOVE:* JIMMIE JOHNSON STRAPS HEAT SHIELDS ONTO THE BOTTOM OF HIS SHOES.

Hot Topics

When race cars crash, the first concern is fire. If a fuel tank bursts and gas is lit, a driver may get trapped in the flames. A fire wall behind the driver protects the driver from the gas tank. A fire extinguisher is right beside the driver for emergencies. If a fire does occur, the driver's suit should be enough protection until help arrives. The suit is made of material that guards against fire. Most drivers also wear special underwear that guards against fire. They also put on special gloves and boots that can prevent burns.

JEFF GREEN LOOKS AT THE HEAT DAMAGE DONE TO HIS CAR AFTER AN ACCIDENT. NASCAR TRACK WORKERS ARRIVED IN SECONDS TO MAKE SURE GREEN WAS SAFE.

Several years ago, NASCAR began developing a car that would have better safety features for its drivers. They called it the Car of Tomorrow (COT). To design the COT, NASCAR's safety experts studied different crashes. Engineers agreed that the driver's seat should be four inches closer to the middle of the car and three inches toward the rear. These changes protect drivers better in crashes. Drivers drove the COT in a couple of races in 2007. By 2008, the new design was in full use.

LEFT: DRIVER JUAN PABLO MONTOYA JOINED THE NASCAR SPRINT CUP SERIES FULL TIME IN 2007. HE HAD DRIVEN IN A COUPLE OF NASCAR RACES IN PREVIOUS YEARS. HE LIKES THE IMPROVED SAFETY OF THE CAR OF TOMORROW (COT). *ABOVE:* BRIAN VICKERS IS SURROUNDED BY SAFETY DEVICES IN THE SEAT OF HIS CAR.

Roll with It

During a bad crash, a car may flip onto its roof or its side. Or another car in the crash may not be able to avoid smashing into the first car. To keep drivers from being crushed, sturdy, padded roll bars surround the driver's cockpit (seating area). The roll bars are strong steel tubes that form a cage around the driver. Since 2008, race cars have added energy-absorbing materials near the roll cage. NASCAR drivers are safe because the great forces of energy that occur during a major wreck go around them, not through them.

Do the Math

It takes three seconds to click in each point of a safety belt. How long does it take to lock into a five-point safety system?

(answer on page 48)

THE COCKPIT OF TONY STEWART'S CAR IS BUILT TO ABSORB THE ENERGY OF A CRASH.

Unlike regular cars, a NASCAR driver's seat is molded around the driver's body to fit snugly. The seat belts worn by NASCAR drivers are also different from those in regular cars. NASCAR uses a system of five or six different belts. Each slips through a guide that is attached to the frame of the car. The belts come together at the driver's chest. It takes a while to buckle up but only a second to unbuckle. The Head and Neck Support (HANS) device at the top of the seat holds the driver's neck and head in place. In high-speed crashes, this device can prevent a broken neck.

Show of Force

When a race car rolls, a driver grabs the steering wheel tightly and waits until the car stops moving. If the car is spinning too fast, the driver may not be able to stay still. Netting across the car's side window keeps the driver safe inside until the car stops.

THERE IS DANGER IN ANY ACCIDENT, BUT NASCAR IS ALWAYS FINDING NEW WAYS TO PROTECT DRIVERS. THANKS TO HIS SAFETY SYSTEMS, RYAN NEWMAN (NO. 12) WALKED AWAY FROM THIS CRASH DURING THE 2003 DAYTONA 500.

See for Yourself

Why are seat belts wide and not thin?
Try this experiment, and you will find out.

• Make two six -inch tall "drivers" out of modeling clay.

• Snip off an eight -inch length of sewing thread. Cut an eight-inch length of two-inch-wide party ribbon. Tie a knot in each length to form two little circles.

• Hold one of the drivers in one hand. Loop the thread around its waist. With your other hand, give a strong tug. The clay cuts in half.

• Hold your other driver. Repeat the action with the thick ribbon. Pull just as hard. Is the driver still in one piece?

The force of the belts must be spread out over a wide area to work correctly. So your clay driver is protected. This is why NASCAR drivers wear five or six wide safety belts when they race.

Head and Shoulders

All NASCAR drivers use the HANS device that protects the head and neck. It is attached to the driver's body, instead of to the seat or the car frame. In the case of sudden forces, this device can stop serious injuries from taking place.

DRIVER JEFF BURTON CHECKS OUT HIS SEAT AND SAFETY HARNESS BEFORE THE 2007 DAYTONA 500.

Shoptalk

"[THE]...COLLAR...FITS BETWEEN THE SHOULDER BELTS AND THE BODY, OVER THE SHOULDERS AND IN FRONT OF THE CHEST. IT'S HELD IN PLACE WITH THE SHOULDER STRAPS."

—DRIVER SCOTT PRUETT (*ABOVE*), DESCRIBING HOW HIS HANS DEVICE WORKS

The science of safety is not limited to the area around the driver. NASCAR also puts a lot of thought into the way cars are built. It's also careful about the way tracks are designed. When an impact occurs at 180 miles per hour, great forces are unleashed. The goal of NASCAR's safety experts is to understand how these forces work and how they can be controlled.

A NASCAR OFFICIAL STANDS AT THE STARTING LINE BEFORE A RACE. CARS ARE INSPECTED BEFORE AND AFTER A RACE.

LEFT: JEFF GREEN (*NO. 30*) HITS THE WALL AT BRISTOL MOTOR SPEEDWAY IN TENNESSEE. HIS CAR AND THE WALL ARE MADE TO ABSORB THE FORCE OF THE CRASH. *BELOW:* A STURDY WALL AND SAFETY SCREEN KEEP THE FANS SAFE AT NASCAR RACES.

Absorbing Energy

The colorful cars you see on race day are built to go fast. They are also designed to keep the driver safe. Every inch of these cars is made to take in the energy of a wreck before it reaches the driver. NASCAR crash experts study each crash and learn from it. When they see a way to protect drivers, they pass along that information to the racing teams. For example, NASCAR recently decided to improve the driver-side doors. They were redesigned to be filled with energy-absorbing foam. All racing teams use them. Teams often share their own safety discoveries too.

In the Mix

The windshields of NASCAR race cars are made of Lexan. This shatterproof material is very strong but also very soft. It can be scratched with a fingernail. Most racing teams put several layers of sticky see-through film over their windshields. The layers become dirty or damaged during a race. The pit crews peel them off, one layer at a time.

A MEMBER OF GREG BIFFLE'S CREW PEELS A LAYER OF FILM OFF THE WINDSHIELD OF HIS CAR.

NASCAR designers know that the most dangerous objects in a crash are jagged or pointy ones. So race cars have no glass, no headlights, and no taillights. Often they don't have side windows. The front and rear windshields are made of plastic that won't shatter. NASCAR has also worked to improve the safety around the gas tank. New types of rubber and steel keep this area from bursting during a wreck.

RIGHT: DAMAGE LIKE THIS WOULD BE MUCH MORE WORSE WITH A GLASS WINDSHIELD. *BELOW:* THE HEADLIGHTS ON THE FRONT OF THIS CAR ARE NOT REAL—A SPECIAL STICKER MAKES THEM LOOK LIKE THEY ARE MADE OF GLASS.

Do the Math

A car starts a race with 12 layers of film over its windshield. The pit crew strips off one layer at each pit stop. The car makes seven pit stops during a race. How many layers are left when the race is over?

(answer on page 48)

Hitting the Wall

When a car skids into a wall, much of the car's energy goes back toward the car and the driver. NASCAR track builders found that they could improve car and driver safety if the walls could take in more of the energy of a crash.

Starting in 2002, NASCAR tracks began installing energy-reduction systems. Every oval-shaped NASCAR track now has them. Some fans call them soft walls. They are special barriers that combine different types of strong materials and flexible foam. When a car hits a soft wall, the wall bends and spreads out the energy from the crash. Less of the energy goes back to the driver or the car.

THE SPACES BUILT INTO THE WALL AT TEXAS MOTOR
SPEEDWAY HELP TO ABSORB ENERGY IF HIT BY A CAR.

TOP: JUAN PABLO MONTOYA
SCRAPES THE WALL AT MICHIGAN
INTERNATIONAL SPEEDWAY. *ABOVE:*
A NASCAR OFFICIAL *(LEFT)* EXPLAINS
HOW A SOFT WALL WORKS.

Shoptalk

"THE IMPACT WASN'T AS BAD AS
I PLANNED FOR….ALL MY SAFETY
STUFF WORKED WELL. THE SOFT
WALL REALLY CUSHIONED
THE IMPACT."

—DRIVER JIMMIE JOHNSON
(LEFT), ON HOW HIS
SAFETY EQUIPMENT
WORKED DURING A
RECENT CRASH

See for Yourself

How do energy-absorbing walls work?
If you still have one of those clay drivers,
find a toy car that it can fit into. Then try
this experiment.

- Ask a grown-up if you can roll your car and driver into a wall either inside or outside your house.
- Stand about six feet away. Give the car a good, strong push. The wall will stop the car suddenly. Did you hear the crunching sound? Did you see what happened to the driver?
- Next, crumple up some newspaper. Stuff it into a grocery bag. Place the bag against the wall. (You can also use a soft pillow.)
- Roll the car and driver into the wall again. Push just as hard (or harder). How is the result different?

With the bag or pillow in place, the energy made by your push is taken in gradually. The impact is spread over a wide area. A real car and driver in this kind of crash would do much better. NASCAR also uses this idea when it designs bumpers and drivers' helmets.

Soft Walls

A lot of science went into inventing soft walls. How well do they work? NASCAR scientists studied accidents at the same tracks, before and after the new walls were put in. They found that soft walls took in a lot more energy. One of the first drivers to test the new design was Jason Keller. He banged into the wall at Richmond International Raceway in Virginia. He walked away uninjured. NASCAR scientist Gary Nelson also liked what he saw. "We realized that wall did so much more than we had ever seen in testing in that type of wreck," he said.

LEFT: SCIENTIST GARY NELSON CHECKS OUT THE INSIDE OF JEFF BURTON'S CAR. NELSON IS ONE OF NASCAR'S TOP SAFETY EXPERTS. *RIGHT:* JASON KELLER WAS GLAD THERE WERE SOFT WALLS AT RICHMOND INTERNATIONAL RACEWAY.

Chapter Five: Always on Call

No matter how careful drivers are or how well racing teams design their cars, things can go wrong. When a driver is injured or when something unsafe is on the track, safety teams step in. Many fans don't think of these people as being part of a race. Ask a driver, and you will hear a different story. Members of safety teams often risk their lives so the drivers don't have to.

TOP: THE SAFETY CREW MAKES SURE THAT MARTIN TRUEX JR. (NEXT TO CAR) IS OKAY AFTER AN ACCIDENT AT ATLANTA MOTOR SPEEDWAY IN GEORGIA. ABOVE: MEMBERS OF THE SAFETY CREW WAVE TO DRIVERS AT THE BEGINNING OF A RACE AT TALLADEGA SUPERSPEEDWAY IN ALABAMA.

Do the Math

A safety crew needs 90 seconds to travel from one end of an oval track through the midpoint of the infield to the other end of the track. Let's say the crew members start in the middle of the infield. How long will it take them to reach a crash during a race?

(answer on page 48)

TOP: A SAFETY VEHICLE PUSHES JOHN ANDRETTI'S CAR OFF THE TRACK AFTER AN ACCIDENT. *ABOVE: A* SAFETY WORKER HELPS DENNY HAMLIN OUT OF HIS CAR AFTER A SPINOUT.

Teamwork

Safety crews work in teams. Some teams are in charge of protecting drivers after accidents. Other teams remove broken cars. A yellow flag being waved at a race means that a caution period has begun. Drivers must slow down and stop passing. Safety crews are sent in to work. The faster they do their jobs, the sooner the race can restart.

NASCAR OFFICIALS HELP GET JEFF GORDON BACK ON THE TRACK AFTER HIS CAR SKIDDED INTO THE INFIELD.

Who are these safety crew members? Some work for NASCAR. Others work for the track. Some are local firefighters, mechanics, and emergency medical staff. All crew members have two things in common. They love racing. They want to make sure drivers and crews are as safe as possible.

ABOVE: SAFETY WORKERS RESPOND QUICKLY TO AN ELECTRICAL PROBLEM IN KEVIN HARVICK'S CAR. *LEFT:* A FIREFIGHTER FROM A NEARBY TOWN WATCHES A RACE AT BRISTOL MOTOR SPEEDWAY. MANY SAFETY WORKERS LIVE AND WORK NEAR THE NASCAR RACE TRACKS.

Do the Math

Let's say a NASCAR medical team is made up of three doctors and four nurses. They are helped by eight assistants. What is the total number of people on the team?

(answer on page 48)

Working Together

NASCAR sends officials to help safety and medical crews at every race. Before a race, these officials spend many hours making sure crews are fully prepared. They explain any changes that have taken place in the cars. The crews must know about all the latest safety devices. If a driver must be helped out of a car after an accident, every second counts. NASCAR officials go to many races. So they can share new ideas with teams at every track. After each race, NASCAR reviews the performance of its safety teams.

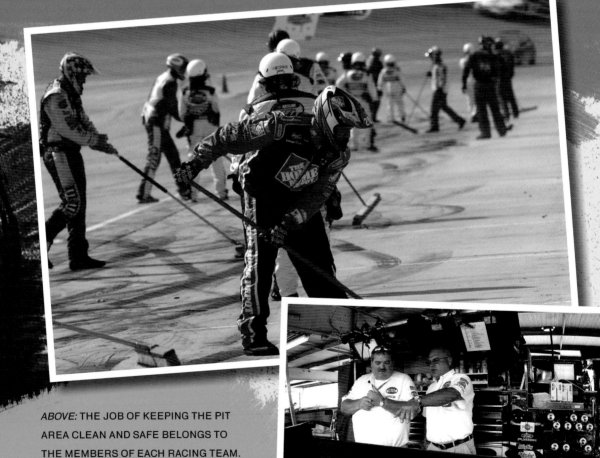

ABOVE: THE JOB OF KEEPING THE PIT AREA CLEAN AND SAFE BELONGS TO THE MEMBERS OF EACH RACING TEAM.
RIGHT: NASCAR OFFICIALS CHECK KENNY WALLACE'S CAR BEFORE A 2007 RACE AT DOVER INTERNATIONAL SPEEDWAY IN DELAWARE.

Do the Math

Most NASCAR safety crews work at three races over a weekend. Each race takes three hours. Let's say NASCAR holds two events a year at the track. How many hours of racing does a safety crew member work each year?

(answer on page 48)

TOP LEFT: SAFETY CREWS MUST WORK FAST WHEN A CAR GETS STUCK ON THE TRACK. *ABOVE:* A NASCAR OFFICIAL WATCHES OVER PIT ROAD.

See for Yourself

How difficult is it to clean up oil on a track?
Until very recently, removing oil entirely
from a track surface was almost impossible.
To understand why, try this experiment.

- Find three hard plastic picnic plates. Use the ones that are flat, without dividers within the plate area. This is your track surface.
- Spread one-half teaspoon of cooking oil on each surface.
- Try cleaning up the first oil puddle with a paper towel or napkin. After 60 seconds, use your finger to check how slick the surface still is.
- Try to clean up the second oil puddle with clean cat litter made of clay. Cover the oil with the litter, and wait 60 seconds. Then brush the litter into a trash can. Check to see how slick the surface is.
- Try breaking down the third oil puddle by squeezing some grease-cutting dishwashing liquid onto a sponge soaked with warm water. Scrub the oil slick. Check to see how slick the surface is.

As you can see, oil is hard to break down. Recently, NASCAR started using a cleanup product that surrounds the oil. This new product cleans the track completely. It also makes the oil safer to get rid of later.

Looking Out for Number One

Once a NASCAR race begins, the most important safety experts are the drivers themselves. They know what their cars can and can't do. They have checked their gear from head to toe. They understand the risks involved in trying to win a race. They know how to act in emergencies. And they trust their fellow drivers to drive safely. A. J. Foyt competed in NASCAR races in the 1960s. He once said he felt safer on a race track than on a highway. Modern NASCAR stars would agree.

Shoptalk

"I THINK ABOUT TRYING TO RELAX AND LETTING THE SAFETY EQUIPMENT DO ITS JOB."

—DRIVER CARL EDWARDS, ON WHAT HE THINKS ABOUT DURING A CRASH

ABOVE RIGHT: JEFF GORDON *(LEFT)* CHECKS HIS ENGINE CAREFULLY BEFORE EVERY RACE.
ABOVE: CARL EDWARDS TRUSTS THE SAFETY EQUIPMENT IN HIS CAR WHEN HE IS IN AN ACCIDENT.

Glossary

air pressure: the weight of air on a race car

block: to slip in front of a car to stop it from passing

cockpit: the section of a race car where the driver sits

concussion: an injury to the brain caused by a sudden, hard blow

energy absorbing: material that takes in and spreads out energy from strong forces

engineer: a person who studies how to build and design machines and structures

friction: the force that slows down objects when they rub against one another

infield: the inner area of an oval track

momentum: the force or speed an object has when it is moving

motor oil: a special liquid that helps engine parts run more smoothly

NASCAR: the National Association for Stock Car Auto Racing

organ: a part of the human body, such as the heart, that works to keep a person alive

physics: the study of how objects in motion behave

pit crew: the seven-member team that takes care of a race car during a race

roll cage: a steel frame inside a race car that protects the driver in case of an accident

safety system: the parts of a car that work together to prevent serious injuries

Learn More

Books

Buckley, James. *NASCAR*. New York: DK Eyewitness Books, 2005.

Buckley, James. *Speedway Superstars*. Pleasantville, NY: Reader's Digest, 2004.

Doeden, Matt. *Stock Cars*. Minneapolis: Lerner Publications Company, 2007.

Fielden, Greg. *NASCAR Chronicle*. Lincolnwood, IL: Publications International, Ltd., 2003.

Savage, Jeff. *Dale Earnhardt Jr.* Minneapolis: Lerner Publications Company, 2006.

Sporting News. *NASCAR Record & Fact Book*. Charlotte, NC: Sporting News, 2007.

Woods, Bob. *The Greatest Races*. Pleasantville, NY: Reader's Digest, 2004.

Woods, Bob. *NASCAR Pit Pass: Behind the Scenes of NASCAR*. Pleasantville, NY: Reader's Digest, 2005.

Website and Video Game

NASCAR
http://www.nascar.com
NASCAR.com is the official site of NASCAR.
From here you can find information on drivers and their teams, as well as previews of upcoming races, schedules, and a look back at NASCAR's history.

NASCAR 2008. Video game. Redwood City, CA: EA Sports, 2008.
With an ESRB rating of E for "everyone," this game gives fans a chance to experience the speed and thrills of driving in a NASCAR race.

Index

Do the Math Answers

Page 8: 3,690 pounds. 3,400 pounds + 180 pounds + 110 pounds = 3,690 pounds.

Page 17: 400 pounds. 150 pounds + 250 pounds = 400 pounds.

Page 26: 15 seconds. 3 seconds x 5 points = 15 seconds.

Page 33: 5 layers. 12 layers – 7 layers = 5 layers.

Page 38: 45 seconds. 90 seconds x ½ = 45 seconds.

Page 41: 15 team members. 3 doctors + 4 nurses + 8 assistants = 15 team members.

Page 43: 18 hours. 3 races x 3 hours x 2 times per year = 18 hours worked per year.